!ONE-GREAT-THING!

"YOU SHOULD DO"

VE SUCCESSFUL-RELATIONSHIPS and A-HAPPY-LIFE.

Rub this book between your hands (THOUGHTS) three times a day and,
You "will" get everything you want . . . to be, do, and have.

Published by:
The Number 2 Pencil Foundation, 501(c)(3)
www.thenumber2pencil.org
Email: thenumber2pencilfoundation@gmail.com

To learn more about the author or his publications please visit:
www.johnsolomonsandridge.com

Cover Art Created by The Black Artist John Solomon Sandridge (aka Immortal Black Boy)

Cover & Interior Design by Daniel Middleton
www.scribefreelance.com

100% of the proceeds from sales of this book are given to The Number 2 Pencil Foundation. Those proceeds are thereafter used to reproduce art-related items created by John Solomon Sandridge and school students. Those art pieces are then donated to schools and libraries . . . in other words, schools and libraries receive them for FREE.

For further information please contact Frances Irene at: (205) 603-4523

ISBN: 978-0-9667336-17 (Hardcover)
978-0-9667336-5-5 (Softcover)

Printed in the United States of America

THIS BOOK AND ME

What is it worth to have relationships that are free of problems—lingering disappointments and nagging regrets? Since the relationships do not cause problems, what does?

For more than 4-decades I invested my time—life—to reading hundreds of books on self-help and Jungian psychology, attended numerous personal-growth workshops, and practiced Intuitive-Naturopathic Body-Brain-Mind healing. Those tireless efforts were rewarded with a truth that had been taught by great teachers of every century: Rather than practicing "be**lie**v**ing**" they taught the importance of "**do***in*g" the *One-Great-Thing* that produces Permanent-Life-Changing-Results.

That *One-Great-Thing* is . . . ***Change Your Attitude.***

Practicing *One-Great-Thing* everyday for 1-year will convert disappointments into *self-forgiveness*, which turns regrets into *forgiving-others*. This success reduces 98% of mental, emotional, psychological, and physical pains.

How do I know? The 41-years I studied and practiced self-healing added up to the *One-Great-Thing*, me **Changing My Attitude**. I gradually understood my attitude was a hidden world of negative-fear-based "what's wrong with other people and the world" beliefs and thoughts. And my mind was writing the plot for the unwanted—movie—life I was living. Since my outer-life was not what I wanted, I had to give the plot writer—my mind—different information: *"what I do want"* and not *"what I don't want."* Those years were pregnant with the need to have **go**od relationships and a better life.

The result of **Changing My Attitude**?: my personal and business relationships are sailing smoothly over the turbulent waters of unconsciousness: blaming others for my personal-problems.

After 4-months of planning and 7-days of writing, this book was birthed. Its simple Attitude-Changing-Practices produces inner-changes which are reflected in outer-life: situations, conditions, and circumstances.

Why bother searching for a purpose? Save time—life. Do *One-Great-Thing*. **Change Your Attitude and** your outer life will automatically match . . . ***Your-nner-World*** . . . ***Your-Attitude.***

Notes

THE MIND THAT BE<u>**LIE**</u>VES

Life is supposed to be filled with suffering leads ***the brain*** to create patterns for suffering, ***the body*** will experience the suffering, and ***the person*** will live in . . . ***suffer****ings*.

Notes

HUMBLING(S)

In the first half of life one is humbled by pain, hurt, and suffering.

In the second half of **life it's healthier** to be **humble**d by appreciation, **thankful**ness, and gr**atitude**.

Notes

BE CARE-*FUL*

What you wish for . . . ***"You will"*** . . . get that.

Notes

BE CONSCIOUS

Of **what** you are w**is**hing for **now** . . . it's . . . happening **in**side **you**.

Notes

WHAT YOU THINK ABOUT MOST

Is *happen**ing*** in **your life** . . . and the world . . . ***now***.

Notes

WHAT YOU *TALK* ABOUT MOST

Is . . . how ***you*** "will" . . . ***always*** . . . live.

Notes

VISUALIZE

Each morning, before **get**ting **out of bed**, see everyone you meet **be**ing **happy and peaceful**.

Notes

YOU *ARE* GOING TO DIE

You were born to do **The One-Great-Thing** . . . ***Be****fore* . . . You Die.

Notes

A COMMERCIAL

THE INTEGRATION-SEPARATION-MEDITATION
10-MINUTES 3-TIMES A DAY

THE FIRST 5-MINUTES:

Sit in a chair, your back straight, and feet flat on the floor. Close your eyes. Relax your entire body. Try to pull the bottom of your shoulder blades together. Hold this position for 22–seconds then gently release. Focus on your inhaling and exhaling breathing. While inhaling ***"feel"*** your **body** and **brain** and **mind** filling with ***"everything"*** on earth, all universes, and all galaxies. While exhaling ***"feel"*** your **body** and **brain** and **mind** separating from ***"everything"*** that ex**is**ts.

THE SECOND 5-MINUTES:

In the same position: focus ***"only"*** on your inhaling and exhaling breathing. When your **mind wonders from thought to** th**ought**, and it will, refocus on your inhaling and exhaling breathing. Refocus as often as necessary.

Notes

NIGHTLY PRACTICE

At bedtime before slipping into sleep *"**see and feel yourself*** greeting everyone ***with a smile**"* (include enemies *and* parents).

Notes

!!!!!IMPORTANT!!!!!

Pr***act***ice ***"Emotional -Intelligence"***: understand when it's best to say no-thing . . . ***Only -Listen***.

Notes

NEVER

Get revenge. "***You*** only hurt" . . . ***more***.

Notes

NOT IMPORTANT!

Always . . . **be**ing . . . ***right***.

Notes

ELIMINATE

The . . . ***"need to"*** be . . . ***right***.

Notes

PR**ACT**ICE

Being ***humble****d* ***every time*** something . . . ***"GOoD" happens to you***.

Notes

BE GRATE**FUL**

Daily. ***Think*** about ***your life*** be***in***g worse than what it is now . . . then . . . 'Give Thanks For What You Have ***This Moment.***"

Notes

BE MORE THAN POS**IT**IVE

Be understanding. Understanding leads to acceptance. Acceptance . . . is . . . ***Healing***.

Notes

S**TOP**

Complain**in**g.

Notes

PROBLEMS

See all problems as opportunities, and discover something beneficial for . . . "**You First Then Others**."

Notes

BE**LI**E**VE**

You are supposed to . . . and will . . . "***make a GOoD-difference in the world.***"

Notes

kNOW

The world **will be** in***complete if you*** die without ***do***ing . . . ***your*** . . . ***One-Great-Thing***.

Notes

DO NOT TRY

To help people who are not asking for y***<u>our</u>*** help . . . ***<u>God Does Not</u>*** . . . ***<u>why</u>*** would ***<u>you</u>***?

Notes

ANOTHER COMMERCIAL

DAILY FLOW

At least ***twice a day***. . . be sure to ***have total*** bowel ***eliminations***.

Notes

DAILY EXERCISES

Stand as much as possible. **Walk** as much **a**s possible. S**mile** **often**.

Notes

DAILY EATING

Never overeat. Never over-drink. (Burp to avoid bursting a gut.)

Notes

RELATIONSHIPS

All during the **day**, every day, **have positive** th**oughts** **about** people . . . you **love** and hate.

Notes

FOR PERSONAL GROWTH

Have **meaningful** ***conversations*** . . . **98% of the day**.

Notes

DAILY THINKING

Eliminate th**oughts about what other people should be and do**. Be what *“**they should.**”*

Notes

ASK 6-**INDIVIDUALS**

What they ***"feel*** you *need* to ***change"*** to be a greater person . . . then . . . Pr***act***ice ***Be***ing-***That***.

Notes

REMEMBER

The GOoD and bad ***"you do*** to and think of others . . . ***is*** . . . com***in***g back to ***you."***

Notes

IN THE END

Everyth***I***ng you have -***A***cco***M***plished came through **re**petition . . . pr**act**ice . . . ***The One-Great-Thing***.

Notes

REAL-POWER

SURRENDER PRAYER

I AM Surrendered:
I surrender my will for Your-Will.
I surrender my thoughts for Your-Thoughts.
I surrender my ways for Your-Ways.

Your-Will be done in me and through me for Your Divine Heavenly-Purpose,
Which is my divine earthly-mission.

I AM thankful.
I AM grateful.
I AM aprec***I***a***T***ive.

So be IT. So IT is.

Amen, A-women, and A-children.

Notes

LAST COMMERCIAL

SO AND IF

This book is beneficial to you purchase copies and give them away. ***"You-Will"*** bring ***"change"*** to others and the earth.

Give a-way 1-copy to anyone, and ***"You-Will". . .*** *A Spiritual-Shift In Your Life.*

Give a-way 11-copies to others, and "***Your-Will***" creates a ***Spiritual-Shift*** in the lives of: family, friends, acquaintances, and strangers.

Giving a-way 22-copies, and the Spiritual-Shift will expand to your city.

Give a-way 44-copies, and the Spiritual-Shift will spread throughout your state.

Give a-way 88-copies, and the Spiritual-Shift will bleed throughout your country.

Give a-way 176-copies, and the Spiritual-Shift will spill into 22-countries.

Give a-way 352-copies, and the Spiritual-Shift will spill into 44-countries.

Give a-way 704-copies, and the Spiritual-Shift will spill into 88-countries.

Give a-way 1,408-copies, and the Spiritual-Shift will spread throughout the world.

100% of the proceeds from sales of this book are given to The Number 2 Pencil Foundation. Those proceeds are thereafter used to reproduce art-related items created by John Solomon Sandridge and school students. Those art pieces are then donated to schools and libraries . . . in other words, schools and libraries receive them for FREE.

Don't take my word . . . Don't even tr***us***t ***me*** . . .

JUST PRACTICE

!ONE-GREAT-THING!

CPSIA information can be obtained
at www.ICGtesting.com
Printed in the USA
BVHW03s1145180418
513722BV00019B/431/P